SUEDE
the beautiful ones

PHOTOGRAPHIC CREDITS

FRONT COVER PHOTOGRAPH © CHRIS FLOYD, © ALL ACTION
© ALL ACTION
© STEVE DOUBLE
© LONDON FEATURES INTERNATIONAL LTD
© ANGELA LUBRANO
© PICTORIAL PRESS
© REDFERNS
© REX FEATURES

UFO Music Ltd 18 Hanway Street London W1P 9DD England
Telephone: 0171 636 1281 Fax: 0171 636 0738

First published in Great Britain 1997
UFO Music Ltd 18 Hanway Street
London W1P 9DD

ISBN 1-873884-80-X

Designed by UFO Music Ltd

Roger Morton

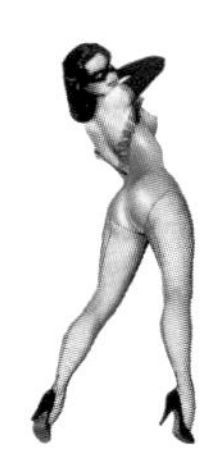

FIEZ-NOUS
TRE BRONZA

suede /*swad*/ [Fr. *sued*], *n.* undressed kid; its colour. - Also *adj.* - *v.t.* to give a suede finish to (leather or cloth). [Fr. (*gants de*) Suede, (gloves of) Sweden.]

chapter one
so young

so young

At the start of the 90s the five letter swirl of s-u-e-d-e was a three line entry in the dictionary with little meaning outside a declining branch of the garment industry. Nobody really wore suede any more. It was three decades on since Elvis had made an issue out of his 'Blue Suede Shoes'. Morrissey's recent use of the obscure Brit youth haircut term 'Suedehead' for an album title was mostly a matter for trainspotters. So the first time the word brushed the eardrums of the gabbling pop world in 1992 it inferred very little except that maybe this was some sort of a faddy, fashion band.

Felt had come and gone causing hardly a ripple. Leatherface were currently eroding the nation's motorways. Nobody had dared to name their imitation grunge band Plaid yet, but it was bound to happen. So Suede would get their fifteen minutes sham of fame. And roll on the circus of shouty low-ambition. What did it matter if Midway Sunk had the depth of a beer mat, as long as they made a loud noise and skateboarded out the picture fast? After a lengthy detour into MDMA fusion, British pop, particularly London based British pop, had seriously low self esteem, and the idea that some clothes horse band called Suede could stretch anybody's imagination further than the creaky front door of the Camden Falcon pub, was impossible to countenance.

History is in danger of forgetting how narrow the pop parameters were getting before Suede came and levered them apart. The rolling momentum of great British bands had ground to a halt with the inactivity of The Stone Roses and a pincer movement of grunge and techno had caused such a degree of phobia about 'popstars' that any form of non-communal self-expression had been virtually outlawed. Pop was in the closet, and until Suede came along with their gauche, self-celebratory extroversion, a subtle boredom was settling on the decade.

Keith Richards once said that the Sixties were monochrome until the arrival of The Beatles and The Stones. They flipped on the polychromatic lights and the party started. Looking back, that's what Suede did for the lost teenagers of the fractured and fizzling 90s. They changed the way everything felt. They lit up the backdrop.

In the summer of 1996 the singer with the lightly named pop group Suede sits at a desk in the Central London offices of his band's record company Nude. He is dressed in everyday black and catwalk thin. The boyish haircut, the petrol blue eyes and the tightly drawn skin enunciate a strangely resonant 90s chic. He looks like some prototype style mag model but his demeanour is sober and unaffected and there's a palpable aura of determination about him. You would think, on meeting Brett Anderson on a sensually warm urban afternoon in mid 96, that he had emerged from some great trial, had been put upon and battered about, had lost himself in protracted mangled consciousness, and had emerged on the other side with a new fire hardened edge. He is lucid to the point of cruelty.

Sucking on a cigarette, he leans back and surveys the mountains of tapes around him. The cramped office belongs to one of Nude's A&R men and the stacks of tapes from hopeful bands resembles the Manhattan skyline. Brett runs his eyes down the scrabble of names and laughs the laugh of someone who's pulled lightyears away from the zoo of interchangeable bands. "Smaller?" he smirks.

"It's not one of those names that inspires confidence is it?" Suede, on the other hand is a name that in the blip of half a decade has become an affirmatory landmark as weighty and looming as London's Centrepoint skyscraper. The word Suede has been sucked out of the dictionary and turned into a reverberating symbol, rallying point, an aesthetic satellite station and according to Brett, a new adjective too.

"Neil was an incredibly Suede person before he even started." He says, talking about the recent arrival in the band of pretty boy keyboard player Neil Codling. The use of the band's name as a descriptive term trips naturally off his tongue.

So Suede is an adjective now? You can be a Suede person?

"A Suede person! Suede people. Yeaaah. But he is! There just are some people that I find are Suede people and other people just aren't."

It's a loose term or course, the constantly evolving 'Suede'. But you could reasonably say that it suggests the following: hard edged romance, sexual crossover, urban chemical euphoria, dark vicious glamour, kitchen sink beauty, operatic scope, cinematic

1

so young

poise, wasted youth, high-speed violence, graphic bliss, caged alienation, a way of holding a cigarette and a form of pride created by a small confederation of outsiders. Suede Pride week is long overdue.

"I was watching this thing about this artist the other day on TV and it struck home," says Brett. **"It was some pop artist sculpture bloke, and they were saying about how his things were always to do with escapism, because he found himself between two things. He was like this immigrant guy, came from somewhere in Eastern Europe, and his stuff was escaping because he didn't feel part of it. I suppose it's the same for me. I thought it was quite applicable really because lots of the things I write about are about escapism, about, not a netherworld, but sort of like the future, and I do try to be very positive about stuff, and it applies to me because I do feel myself sort of caught between....".**

His voice trails off into silence.

See you in your next life when we'll fly away for good
Stars in our own car we can drive away from here
Far away, so far away down to Worthing and work there
Far away, we'll go far away and flog ice creams
'til the company's on it's knees...
('The Next Life')

chapter two
pantomine horses

Brett Lewis Anderson was born in Haywards Heath on September 29 1967, facing a future as an ice cream man or in the dreams of his father, a classical pianist. His parents lived on a council estate at the Lindfield end of the small commuter town and there was already one four year old child in residence, Brett's sister Blandine. It was according to Anderson, a subtilely constricting childhood. Hayward's Heath is generally perceived as little more than a subliminal flash as travellers hurtle past on the Gatwick branch of the train from London to Brighton. It does however possess a certain golfing classes reputation for comfortable living and the young Anderson grew up feeling excluded.

In his own assessment, Brett was neither working class nor middle class, but "a bit of a satellite". Certainly his family was by no means wealthy. His grandfather had died an alcoholic on a park bench and his father Peter Anderson was out of work for most of Brett's childhood. During the swinging 60s, the Andersons had kept out of the cultural upheavals of the time and developed their own sidestreet bohemian lifestyle. Peter Anderson was an avid classical music fan who kept the house swaying to the music of Berlioz, Mahler, Tchaikovsky and particularly Franz Listz. Blandine was named after one of Listz's daughters and every year Peter would make a pilgrimage to the flamboyant Hungarian's birthplace where he would kiss the ground. In addition to his Listz-o-mania, Peter was greatly enamoured of Churchill and Nelson (mysteriously, Brett was even born on the same day as the Admiral), and would hang a Union Jack outside the house on their birthdays.

Nowadays Brett Anderson expresses pride in his father's eccentricities. As a teenager, however, he was less amused. While his old man drifted in and mostly out of work as a swimming pool attendant and ice cream man (nowadays he drives a taxi) Brett began to develop his own artistic side. His empathy lay in the direction of his painter mother and as a kid he painted his own murals on his bedroom wall - Dennis The Menace, Bob Dylan and The Beatles.

From his early teenage years pop music was a tool. While his dad played Berlioz downstairs Brett would turn up Crass and Discharge punk records upstairs. In his punk phase he hacked his hair off to look "like something that had survived a laboratory experiment." The search for teen identity was more than averagely pronounced in Brett. He processed options at speed. At 12 he wrote his first Beatles inspired song (he later recalled it as 'Positively Negative' although the title might sound familiar to Oasis fans) on an acoustic guitar. And there was an early dabbling with drugs, taking acid in the local park and climbing to the top of a building site out of his head on mushrooms.

Despite being good at sports to the extent of holding his school's 800m track record for five years, Brett was clearly cutting away from the local crowd. His sister was attending art college in Worthing and Brett would occasionally visit her, relishing the strange ambience of boho life mixed with the flavours of seaside retirement homes. Blandine had been a David Bowie fan, and Brett adopted the records adding a taste for Bowie to his own love of Kate Bush. By the mid 80s he had bleached his hair, bought a yellow Cliff Richard suit and was strolling the streets of Haywards Heath, a canary toreador taunting the twitching lace curtains. The suburbs were fascinating but repellent and as the trains rushed past on their way to London Brett would watch and wonder about a more vital life.

"I was obsessed by fame because I felt completely excluded from it," he recalled later.

The doorways started to open while Brett was still at Oat Hall Comprehensive. After having seen him around town in his flamboyant suits, schoolmate Mat Osman edged into the arty crowd that Brett hung out with.

"Brett was different even at school," Mat told Vox in May 93. **"He was a well known face around town. I knew of him before I knew him because he was an oddity. The first time I met him he was wearing a pink suit, a raincoat, and had on a shirt and tie with a tie-pin. And he had a long legged girl hanging on his arm."**

The tall and dependable Mat was as much into music as Brett was and together they would travel down to Brighton to check out bands and particularly to feast on the only 80s group to mean anything to them - The Smiths. Fans from the start, they had recognised Morrissey as a fellow outsider. To

Brett, who's girlish looks had singled him out as a "queer" throughout his teenage years, and who'd regularly been beaten up as a consequence, Morrissey's poetic flaunting of hazy gender affiliation looked like an appealing form of revenge.

In 1985, Brett and Osman formed their first band, a three piece called Geoff, fronted by local boy Gareth Perry. With the pink suited Brett on rudimentary guitar they got as far as a gig at the local town hall and promptly split up. Perry figured they were going nowhere. Mat and Brett, however had other ideas. The ashes of Geoff reinvented themselves as a clangorous Goth rock band - Paint It Black. A short lived affair Paint It Black was also condemned to the cemetery of try out bands and they played out their Sixth Form musical careers as Suave And Elegant.

While Brett was not a bookish student he studied enough to get by. His disinterest in books is still with him today, but back then he spent enough time in the library to clock up three C grade A levels in Maths Chemistry and Physics. An initial foray into academia took him to Manchester University, but despite the city's rich musical past (home to the Smiths, Fall, Roses, Joy Division) he lasted a mere two weeks on his Town And Country Planning course. A brief stint DJ'ing in a Manchester club, slipping in Bowie tunes amongst the disco fodder, and getting bottles thrown at him for his pains, didn't last much longer.

The 19 year old Brett wound his way back down South and relocated to London where he was theoretically studying Planning at London University College. There were, however, distractions. His musical campadre Mat was attending The London School Of Economics and for both of them, student life was mostly a pretext for getting a functioning band together. Suave And Elegant still existed as a possibility and when Brett met and fell for UCL student Justine Frischmann - subsequently known to the tabloids as Justine from Elastica - a third member was added to the embryo band.

Brett now had a rhythm guitarist and a

girlfriend. He changed his course to Architecture, which just happened to be the same subject Justine was studying, and for three years, through a succession of low rent rooms around Edgware, Tottenham Court Road and Finsbury Park they shared the double-edged wonder of downbeat city student life. Parties, clubs, drugs, second hand clothes, band practice and "sitting round a candle in a gruesome house in Finsbury Park". Brett even scraped through his degree. **"I did a couple of drawings of houses one night at 2 o'clock in the morning,"** he recalls.

Their tutors might have thought they were dossing about but the roots of Suede were busy sucking up the glimmer and grime of the mad old, wrecked old, beautiful old city around them. A vision of London, long a place of fantasy for Brett, was forming. **"Life in two rooms in London can be fascinating, absurd, beautiful, glamourous,"** Mat told Select in 1992.

After five years of experiencing the view from a soot smeared one bed, he was by then something of an authority, as was Anderson who made a point of telling early interviewers of his affection for the "steaming mass of brilliant terrible people". The old smoke had got into their veins. Now they just had to get some of it on record.

By 1989 the drum machine backed trio of Anderson, Osman and Frischmann had changed their name to Suede, partly out of admiration for the appellational cool of mid-Eighties Creation band Felt (who were themselves the truncated inheritors of The Velvet Underground's epithet style). In October of that year they placed an advert in the NME,

> *"Young guitar player needed by London based band. Smiths Commotions Bowie PSB. No musos please. Some things are more important than ability. Phone Brett..."*

According to Osman the true birth of Suede took place when the first person to reply to the ad walked through the door. It was a nineteen year old guitarist called Bernard Butler.

The third son of an East London Irish Catholic family, Butler was skinny and shy but completely devoted to his instrument. After six years learning the violin he gave up because he couldn't stand being told how to play. One of his brothers guitars proved to be a better option. He could freeform like a demon and immerse himself completely. Again, it was The Smiths who provided the trainee musician with a template, or more specifically their guitarist Johnny Marr. Butler was a devoted fan, following the Mancunians progress through each guitar and buying his own cherry red Les Paul in homage.

If Anderson's extrovert tendencies made him an ideal frontman, then Butler's in-turned, guitar channelled ardour was the perfect six string accompaniment. Osman remembers him as a strange mixture of diffidence and arrogance on that first meeting.

Having ensured his place in the band with a fierce performance, Butler reverted to his Queens College history student persona and backed out of the room sheltering behind his guitar case. But before he left he made a point of asking Brett and Osman their ages. **"Erm, 23,"** they mumbled. Butler shot them a scathing glance and replied **"You'd better get a move on then hadn't you"**. The central tension of early Suede was in place. Decadence and fanaticism were on speaking terms.

In the year that Butler joined the band Brett's mother died

of cancer. For all that his musical project was making creative progress there were plenty of dark days in the calendar over the next year and a half. Justine's presence in the band had been undermined by the arrival of Bernard and eventually she left, pointing out years later that, **"if you're playing second guitar with Bernard there's not a lot of room for you to do anything. It wasn't fun near the end."** The gigging life of the infant Suede was none too fulfiling either. For all that Brett recalls **" a funny little honeymoon period. We were going quite well for a while with our drum machine and colourful tops"** the avant punk experiments of that line up pulled in few punters.

The official first ever show was on March 10th 1990 at The White Horse pub in West Hampstead supporting the Prudes and Ruby Tuesdays in front of 20 people. The crowds didn't exactly flock. On thinly attended nights at The Bull And Gate , The Amersham Arms or The Powerhaus in Islington, the drum machine would frequently break down. An early Melody Maker review accused Brett of looking like kids TV presenter Andy Crane and the rest of the band like John Craven. Perhaps it was the baggy denims, garish tee shirts and maracas. Madchester had happened and despite gaining some width in their trousers the somewhat arty young Suede did not fit into the Northern yobs on drugs climate created by the rise of The Happy Monday and The Stone Roses. Their only option was to retreat, leaving to posterity their one early success, a track called 'Wonderful Sometimes' which won Gary Crowley's GLR demo clash five weeks running. The Powerhaus club put the track on their 'What The World Is Waiting For' compilation and Suede hung back in the wings.

Activity in the 90/91 period was distinctly sporadic. Brett hardly had the money to feed his cat let alone contribute to funding band activities. But in October 1990 their hopes were raised when they signed a deal with a tiny Brighton label run by a friend of Mat's. In need of a proper drummer they again put an advert in the music press and to the bands amazement

Smiths drummer Mike Joyce replied. Wary of turning into 'the ones with the Smiths drummer' a permanent alliance was avoided but Joyce played on the 'Be My God' A-side of the planned single, and helped out as a 'fatherly' presence thereafter.

Suede would however have to wait a full year and a half for their vinyl debut. 50 white label copies of 'Be My God'/'Art' were pressed up but a dispute with the label owner who wanted them to sign a seven album deal meant that the single was never released. It was a frustrating year and a half for the band. Mat's flat mate at the time Justin Welch had been filling in occasionally on drums. In June 1991 they met up with Stratford On Avon ex-punk and full on Clash fan Simon Gilbert selling tickets at London's ULU venue. Welch drifted off to a future as Elastica's drummer and Gilbert's 12 bands worth of experience sat down at the Suede drum stool. The classic line up was complete - Brett/Bernard /Mat/Simon - but the national zeitgeist was too busy grooving along to anything with an Andy Weatherall re-mix.

The months ground by and the foursome would sit around Brett's cluttered bed-sit listening to records and figuring out what made Bowie and Beatles songs so effective. Gradually they honed their style and shaded in the set list in what proved to be a vital period of learning. **"Before this we'd write a set of Lilac Time type B-sides and think they were good songs,"** pointed out Bernard.

As they re-aligned the live show to include 'The Drowners', 'He's Dead', 'To The Birds', 'Pantomime Horse' and 'C'mon C'mon C'mon' the distance between Suede and the indie herd widened into a gaping chasm. The Madchester bands were losing momentum but the mostly Southern reply, the hazy and apologetic 'shoegazing' scene was no more in sync with Butler and co. The likes of Ride, Chapterhouse and Slowdive were busy feeding their guitars through racks of effects processors to construct kaleidoscopic mists of sound. The home counties were suddenly dotted with these 'cathedrals of sound' and Suede with their sonic clout based firmly in Bernard's naturally overdriving Vox Ac 30 amps were way too profane to be allowed in. Bernard's attitude was clear.

In a rare interview in Guitar magazine he told Michael Leonard **"These sort of bands look like they've just got out of bed when they play on stage and have untidy bedrooms - and I've always liked a tidy bedroom, y know, ha ha!' "**

The disgusted silence which greeted their 1991 ULU show supporting the Scots boogie bunch Teenage Fan Club was not unusual. They were pouring pop charisma and jagged hauteur into a vat of sludge rock and sooner or later something had to be displaced.

"I think everyone had forgotten about the art of songwriting," says Brett. **"I think we were the first band for along time to re-address the whole songwriting thing. There was a dreadful collection of very average indie music going on and we dragged things from the past and revived the ghost of songwriting and that's something that's definitely been taken on now and it's a good thing. Back then they were all obsessed with the sort of things that real people don't listen to, and that's why indie music became this ghetto and now it's got into the mainstream because it's got a lot better. And that's why we stuck out like a saw thumb because we were the first band for a while that knew what being in a band was supposed to be about."**

By now Brett was firmly embedded in the small Notting Hill flat on the first floor of a Victorian mansion block which he shared with his close friend Alan Fisher. The rock bachelor pad contained a green velvet sofa, a mattress for a bed, a few Bowie posters and a piano which his cat would parade along, composing its own avant garde symphonic poems. Brett's mind might have been focussed on the essentials of songwriting, but when Suede finally flipped out of their chrysalis into public view, it was as much their stylistic difference that caught people's attention. In 1991the almighty success of Nirvana's 'Smells Like Teen Spirit' had turned grunge into mainstream fashion. Slacker chic and testosterone angst were hogging the centre stage. So when Suede turned up sounding like they'd swan dived from Mars and looking like four thrift shop Bryan Ferrys you could hear a pin drop.

At a start of 92 New Year's Eve party they'd met early manager John Edymann who took them on alongside Spitfire. No-one took much notice of their January NME 'On Night' gig at the New Cross Venue but by February word had got round that they were worth watching. The 25th of that month saw them playing with The Werefrogs at the Camden Falcon before a sizeable crowd which included Morrissey, Suggs and reviewers from both the weekly music papers. Morrissey was seen to be taking notes of the lyrics during 'My Insatiable One' and the reviews that came from that night were the most positive yet. The NME went so far as to say that Brett was "as sexily crumpled as an unmade bed on a Sunday morning".

The cat was out of the guitar case and the speed of evolution accelerated. The week after the Falcon gig they recorded 'The Drowners' and on March 10th picked a record deal from the rush of offers. Eschewing long term packages, they signed a two single deal with Nude, the new indie label set up by ex major label A&R man and huge T Rex fan Saul Galpern. In the same week Melody Maker's then assistant editor Steve Sutherland gave them an ecstatic live review for their show at The Powerhaus.

Suddenly Suede were a name to drop. The buzz was rising in pitch, but the final coming out party was yet to come. By now they'd been taken on by the unreasonably

enthusiastic PR team of Savage And Best. Gambling on their uniqueness their press officer Phil Savidge sent the only existing demo of their songs to Steve Sutherland at Melody Maker and Sutherland took a deranged but inspired decision.

Sometime in the week preceding April 25th 1992, Brett and Mat were strolling down Tottenham Court Road when they caught sight of something that stopped them in their tracks. The pair of them stared at the news stand in disbelief. They'd been warned that it might happen but they weren't sure they wanted it. Sutherland had gone ahead and put them on the cover of Melody Maker. Without having released a record, Suede were on the front cover of a national music paper. The banner headline read 'The Best New Band In Britain'.

Sex, drugs, glam-rock, fun, sodomy and flash wing collared shirts - the floodgates of pop melodrama had opened. Suede hit the media like ET landing on Broadcasting House. The first interview proper with Sutherland contained enough sexually provocative statements to fill the letters pages for weeks. Brett wanted a song about a bizarre sexual experience in the top 10, he wanted people to escape into the real world, he wanted to use music to talk about extreme emotions, to talk about 'the used condom' and not 'the beautiful bed'.

It was a graphic entrance and against the backdrop of band's full of good blokes or LSD fantasising Home Counties mutes, it was virtually pornographic. With the aid of a good deal of selective quoting Anderson's mouth formed a latex gold frame around the music. Immediately it was established that 'The Drowners' was about the drug-like intensity of a sexually obsessive relationship, 'My Insatiable One' was partly inspired by the concept of male inflatable dolls and 'Pantomime Horse' was humourously concerned with gay sex. The twin cheek of landing a national music paper front cover before releasing a single note, and then apparently coming on all randy in the (sexual) underworld dropped a cleaver into the spectrum of opinion.

Suede were immediately (intentionally) either hated or loved and their April 28th show at the Covent Garden Africa Centre turned into a media scrum with half the music industry trying to squeeze into a narrow hall just so they could hold an opinion on Brett's arse-slapping antics. It seemed impossible that an actual Suede record could live up to the fuss but when their first Nude release finally arrived, clothed in a gender gameplaying sleeve depicting the model Veruschka body-painted as a man, the contents were perfectly extraordinary.

'The Drowner's was an extravagant, jarring, thrusting, teenage swoon of a record. It had scarfs round it's wrist. Brett's sung in an outrageously mascara'd Cockney accent. And the chorus 'You're taking me ov-aaaah" was instantly on every mimics lips. Clearly it was no longer possible to imagine Suede as part of posited 'Glam Scene' alongside Adorable and The Verve. They were out there on there own and the Venusian cool of accompanying tracks 'My Insatiable One' and 'To The Birds' confirmed it.

"Our history seems to be this catalogue of having to prove stuff all the time which gets quite boring really," reflects Brett. "From the very start we've had this 'up against it' sort of thing, having to prove it, because we've had quite a lot of hyperbole written about us, and when someone writes hyperbole about you and when a whole group of people expects something it's quite criminal to let them down really. It's like that old cliche that you don't let yourself down. The reason the hyperbole existed in the first place is because of the high standards that you set yourself. That's just the way it is.

"You start in the business and you're wide eyed about everything, like a kid in a sweet shop. You're walking around and everything wonderful. There's no sense of the cynicism that accompanies lots of the business, so you do everything as a kind of a laugh, and it's only later that you think 'Fuck. I shouldn't

have done that'. And it does sort of close you up. You go through a period of being really constricted by everything and not letting yourself go. And then you go through that and learn how to deal with it and get the best out of it and still have a bit of control about what you're doing. It's important to get over that, you can't be too precious and too hung up about things."

Learning to deal with the mixed blessing of notoriety was something of a crash course for Suede. Like any band they had wanted the attention and were happy to benefit from it. But they were still disturbed to discover how uncontrollable their 'public image' was.

"The media's so powerful because people remember those things, the headlines and the pictures," observes Brett. "And no-one bothers reading between the lines at the end of the day. For the majority of people music journalism might as well be just that."

Suede's Faustian pact with the press turned what would otherwise have been a steady rise into a hyperbolic curve. Released on May 11th 'The Drowners' went straight to number one in the indie charts above The Mega City Four, The Family Cat and Mudhoney and stayed there for a month. At the end of the year it was also number one in most critics charts of the year's best record, replacing the previous year's choice, Primal Scream's 'Higher Than The Sun' and making a significant point as it did so.

Pre-Suede it was widely assumed that after two Ecstasy fuelled Summers Of Love, 'the kids' had turned into a blissed out lumpen proletariat whose lives could be adequately soundtracked by trance techno, imported two dimensional angst bands or 'Come Together' style druggy bonding tunes. It was that train of thought which produced the number one 1992 hit The Shamen's 'Ebeneezer Good' with it's jolly pro-Ecstasy chorus. What Suede did was to embody the overlooked truth that there was a whole other group of kids who's lives were nothing to do with bouncing up and down in a field, but who had complex dreams and dramatic emotional, sexual and pharmacological lives. Suede's stylistic differences might have made them notorious but it was their connection with a particular urban/suburban reality that made them important. They were a band who really meant something.

""It's just this romance I've got with the whole idea of suburbia," Brett told Andrew Mueller in Melody Maker. **"It actually does spark a little fire in me whenever I see anything connected with it, I don't know why. The ... greyness of it excites me for some reason. It could be the twitching curtains. The respectability hiding something else, maybe that's it.. It's just a desire to talk about those people really. I used to do voluntary work for this community centre and there were all these housewives that used to trundle in with their handicapped kids and their mascara would be running because they'd spent the whole morning crying and the only escape they had was to get a load of Valium down them"**

The recognition factor was massive in Suede.There was an instinctive connection between the suburban bus shelter alchemy of Suede and their fans own aspirations. The kids were not all blankly on one. The desire to "escape into your own life" was general. A whole mass of youth was living in vivid suburbia, traipsing the city on the dole, taking cheap drugs and thinking dirty thoughts. Even the 'fashion' side of Suede which was seen as a consciously retro image was an organic aspect of the band's (and by extension the fans) lives. As Brett pointed out, they were not wearing 70s clothes due to the advice of a svengali stylist, they were wearing them because they were cheap and because it takes a decade for fashion gear to make it into the second hand shops. They were dressed by economics and musically styled by environment. Even the 70s echoes in their sonic imprint was a natural Oedipal journey for a generation born in the 70s and raised with the radio on.

"An important group represents a reflection of people's lives beyond music" Brett told Lime Lizard in 92 and though some might have thought that lending Suede importance after one record was a bit hasty, there was a trade taking place. Suddenly London was a dramatic place to live. The band took a line from 'He's Dead' -

I have the look of a son
With all the love and poison of London

- and turned it into a tee-shirt slogan which floated along the city's street's throughout the summer of 92. 'ALL THE LOVE AND POISON OF LONDON' . Everyone knew what that meant.

Suede's contention that you didn't have to travel far or start hallucinating to find drama and excitement - that it was all right there on the litter clogged, used condom strewn streets - was being vividly demonstrated by the band themselves. Their own backstreet lives were being transformed by drama and scandal. After clocking up their first TV performance, flouncing through 'The Drowners' on the Late Show they headed out on a May UK tour with Kingmaker. It was the wrong time to have Suede as your support band and Loz from Kingmaker suffered from being thrown up against the buzz band of the moment. Reviews fell at Suede's

feet and by the time they were back in London to play the 100 Club on their own, fan hysteria was such that Brett was unable to get through a show without getting his shirt ripped off.

The inconsistencies in their lives were considerable at this point. Between bouts of getting his clothes torn up, Brett continued to live in his Notting Hill one bed, and even signed up for singing lessons at the local adult education centre, where he'd be called upon to sing 'The Phantom Of The Opera' in front of 30 aspiring choral society members. Meanwhile word filtered back from the States that Morrissey had been including 'My Insatiable One' in his live show, and when Suede covered The Pretenders 'Brass In Pocket' for NME's Ruby Trax tape, Brett got to hang out with Chrissy Hynde. The festival season saw the band playing at Reading ("I've never slept in a tent in my life!" Brett quipped to one journo) sounding a deth knell for the shoegazers by pulling in 3000 people to the Melody Maker tent at the same time as Ride were on the main stage.

In September they released second single 'Metal Mickey' backed with 'Where The Pigs Don't Fly' and 'He's Dead' and found themselves negotiating the British Pop initiation ceremony of a Top Of The Pops appearance in a drunken haze. Phonogram had sent them up a congratulatory stash of Jack Daniels and they swaggered through a splendidly degenerate

performance Brett singing the "Oh dad she's driving me mad" refrain from half way into hysteria.

'Metal Mickey might have stopped at No 17 in the national charts but they were still pleased to smuggle a song which concerned itself with *"sex reduced to offal or something, the reduction of love to surgery"* into the living rooms of suburbia.

Suede were natural provocateurs, and not all the responses they provoked were from upset TV viewers. As far back as Autumn '92 the rivalry between Brett and Blur's Damon Albarn was bubbling under.

"They (Suede) specialise in the cocky the camp and the incisive; actually something we've been doing for some time,"commented Damon to Melody Maker.**"His accent is also somewhat similar to mine"** By this time Damon was of course going out with Brett's ex-girlfriend, Justine Frischmann.

The over wrought tone to the year continued with fanatical scenes on an October British tour and a bidding war between American companies trying to sign up Suede outside Britain. Geffen flew them to L.A. and offered in the region of £6 million, but the band thought about it, went sight seeing on Malibu

Beach, came home and signed to Sony for the rest of the world. They now had the corporate might of Sony backing up Nude Records and an expectant public waiting for the debut album. Brett however recalls the second half of 92 as a stormy period of adjusting to being fully sucked into the music business. He was starting to lose touch with old friends and disappear into a band schedule which had included interviews and photo-shoots for 19 magazine front covers in the first year.

By the end of 92 attempts to back out of the limelight and concentrate on the album were being made. No interview was given for the NME Christmas cover where Brett appeared dressed as Sid Vicious in the 'My Way' video. However a Melody Maker round table debate with Brett, Boy George and Lesley Rankine from Silverfish chatting to journos about sex, shoved him more into the spotlight than ever. After explaining the technique of keeping the gender focus in songs open by using 'He' as opposed to 'She', a journalist asked precisely what Brett's point of view was. **"I see myself as a bisexual man who's never had a homosexual experience. That's the way I approach my songwriting,"** he replied. Immediately the quote was seized upon as a generalised statement on his sexuality and for the next two years no Brett interview was complete without referring to it.

Later on Anderson defended himself from charges of '*using* gay imagery'. **"It depresses me because my friends go through emotional turmoil,"** he said. **"I've felt that on their behalf and written songs for them."**

The scandal over the quote is a microcosm of Suede's problems with interpretation. Anderson had always been clear that "twisted sexuality" was something that interested him. The straight Athena postcard/Madonna representation of sex seemed fake to him. Plus in the earlier days he'd spent time hanging out at gay clubs like London's Heaven, half his friends were gay and he'd grown up being positioned as a 'queer' by the town lads. As a writer he just assumed the

ONFIEZ-NOUS
OTRE BRONZAG
LANCASTER

right to slip into whatever persona he wanted. To the militant gays who wrote into the music press, and to the homophobes looking for a cheap laugh he was however, just posing. There wasn't much Anderson could do about the scepticism. It became a fact of life that his sincere attempts to give voice to a divergent sensibility would be seen from the outside as 'tactics'.

"You can't fake anything in this game," says Brett. "It's a sort of popular misconception that bands fake everything, and fake their image and fake their attitude. You can fake it for a space of about two months and then that's it. You always have to be what you are pretty much and the music has got to be pretty much tied up with you personality and how you live your life, otherwise it becomes incredibly false."

Do you think presenting yourself as sexually ambiguous early on lead to you being marginalised?

"It's definitely true. We did marginalise ourselves in that way, but there's nothing I can do anything about. I can't write in a different way. That's where I think the honesty of the band that I've always felt has been there lies. It's been ignored or seen in a completely different light. But it's always been there. It's impossible for me to write in a particular way just to fit in. I just don't write like that. And yeah our whole stance on life is unfashionable but what can you do? It's like, my face looks like this, what can I do about it? This is the way am. I talk this way. My toes are funny. There's very little you can do about it."

The instinctive Suede, (in their public guise as the artifice swathed Suede) kept the pace up throughout 1993. Despite the preposterous omission of their not being nominated in the Best

Newcomer's category they put on a haughty display of feedback'n' swagger for their The Brit Awards Ceremony appearance. And in February with new manager Charlie Charlton on board, their third single the 'Animal Nitrate' (b/w 'Painted People' and 'The Big Time') cruised to number 7 in the charts. It was a kind of scandalous double whammy for the band. Brett got a song with allusions to rough gay sex into the top 10 and at the same time added fuel to growing speculation about his drug use.

The title plays on the gay clubber's drug Amyl Nitrate, and in explaining where the song came from Brett gave interviewers a frank explanation. The backdrop to the song was a cocaine and Ecstasy phase where drugs were replacing people in his life. For Brett it was just a matter of being honest. It certainly wasn't a 'ravehead' mentality coming out. He was more into altered states type drug use - even if it just meant sitting at home on E. The fascination with pills had always been there and sometimes he reckoned his songwriting even benefited from his experiences.

"Whenever I talk about things like that I don't say it for a sense of controversy at all," says Brett. **"Which is what alot of people misread. The serious critics get hold of it they think it's controversial, maybe because it's not part of their live's. But when drugs or any sort of off the wall lifestyle is actually part of your life and part of your friend's lives, then it's just... life. It's not trying to be big or clever or 'God isn't everything incredibly cool and I'm living in this Velvet Underground fantasy', it's just the way it is. It's not that incredible. It's just you got to clubs and everyone's taking drugs and having sex and that's just the way it is, and it doesn't seem particularly controversial."**

But Brett's perspective and the pseudo-morality of the media were not exactly in sync. A gossipy fuss followed his matter of fact comments, and it was almost overlooked that in the February

NME interview with John Mulvey, Simon Gilbert came out as a gay man. The presence of Gilbert in the band didn't however help the censors take a realistic view of the video for 'Animal Nitrate' which was banned from the Chart Show because it showed scenes of men kissing.

In the run up to the release of the debut album Brett's profile continued to climb. The February tour with Pulp and St Etienne kicked off rumours of 'lifestyle' tension between Bernard Butler and Brett. Butler was still resolutely not talking to the press but observers had witnessed his growing impatience with Anderson's public pre-eminence. And as soon as the tour was over another mini-scandal surfaced when Brett's comments about Morrissey made to Amy Raphael in a Face interview ("He's like some kind of useless teenager") got him into a temporary slanging match with his former avatar.

With the album imminent there was a danger that the personality phenomenon of Brett was going to push the music into the background. Anderson was well aware of this. In March he met with his childhood hero David Bowie for an NME front cover piece overseen by Steve Sutherland. The pair talked about stardom, bisexuality and AIDs and Anderson stressed how much he wanted to play live in order to cut through the media overkill. **"I'd never wanna appear like a media fabrication, which I'm sure lots of people think we are,"** he said.

Brett needn't have worried. When 'Suede' the album was unveiled on March 29th, it was strong enough to wipe away all doubts about their depth. Feverish and shimmying, swishy and spunk stained 'Suede's 11 tracks were a deeply precocious placing of low life within the inverted commas of high style. The vocals trilled, the guitars revved and the pianos chimed through 'So Young' and 'She's Not Dead', swinging from the chandeliers for the orchestral 'Sleeping Pills' and waltzing out on the falsetto sigh of 'The Next Life'. The singles rocked, the ballads keened and 100 000

people rushed out and bought it in the first week taking it straight to Number One in the charts. The press might have struggled with the concept of crappy council house lives made magical in song but the discerning public did not.

"It's easy to sit and moan isn't it, to sit there going 'Everything's dreadful'," reflects Brett. **"I find the whole idea of being relentlessly grim about stuff is just too easy. It's like in music that whole thing of these dreadful bloody low-fi American bands moaning about how fucked up they are and shit. I mean who isn't fucked up? Who hasn't got all these problems? There's not anyone in the world, but it's just too easy to say that. And the tricky part of life, the tricky part of music too, is making something great out of all the shit you have to deal with. The truly great musicians, politicians, painters, whatever, deal with all that, and then turn it round and make something good themselves, which I've always tried to do. It's always the way I've written. One of the beauties of writing songs, is that you can take negative stuff, all the shit you have to deal with and turn it into something good. Lots of my early songs, something like 'He's Dead' or 'The Next Life' deal with quite sad subjects, but the fact that you can take these subjects and turn them into something you can get pleasure from is quite a beautiful thing."**

I guess it's that thing of being in the gutter and staring up at the stars.

"Exactly. It's very true. It's one of the things that runs through a lot of Suede and just runs through the way I think about things."

'Suede' was an album of jacked up romance. Quite how much of the skewed love drama related

to Brett's history with Justine was strangely overlooked at the time. But then Elastica's rise was still a long way off and there were other distractions. The sleeve of two women kissing (taken from 'Stolen Glances' a book of lesbian photography published in the 70s by Tee Corrine) aroused more comment. If the band had been allowed to publish the full uncropped picture of two naked women, one in a wheelchair, no doubt the SAS would've been sent in.

Already the band were starting to experience paranoia inducing levels of attention. Brett was finding it hard to leave his house without getting hassled and not everybody was friendly. Rumours and lies spiralled around them, much of it focusing on Brett's relationship with drugs. The cocktail of sex substances and starry eyed tunes was a dangerous one, but it was undeniably effective. In April the band's planned shows at Kilburn National were cancelled when too many tickets were sold for the venue's capacity. Next single 'So Young' (b/w 'Dolly' and 'High Rising') went to 22 in the charts in May and the band played two frenzied shows at the Brixton academy which were filmed by ace face young director Wiz for the 'Love And Poison' video.

There's a scene in 'Love And Poison' where five kids write the word SUEDE by pissing on a wall. From a British perspective it looks like a funny punky teenage gesture. As an image for American MTV it would be pissing incomprehensibly in the wind. The big question for Suede, once they'd triumphed at home with their debut album, was whether they could make it in America. Press favoured British bands had a lousy track record in recent years. The Smiths had only reached large cult level. The Stone Roses had fallen before the first touring hurdle. Unless you were The Cult (or within gothing distance of Depeche Mode) it was going to be an uphill struggle.

"The US is a thing to be broken like a disobedient child" said Brett before getting on the plane. A few weeks later he was back to premier new tune 'Still Life' at the band's Glastonbury headlining slot. **"I didn't realise how infected with fashionable anti-Americanism I was until I went there."** he said. **"It's a 24 hour laugh."**

Clearly some opinions had been revised. The first Suede tour of America was enjoyable enough at least for Brett. They played introductory shows at 300-1000 capacity venues, picked up a committed mini-following, played a huge KROQ festival in L.A. and did the Tonight TV show with Bryan Ferry grooving along in the audience.

From the outside they had every reason to be optimistic about returning to the States later in the year. Their July AIDs benefit show at The Clapham Grand won them alot of friends at home. Chrissy Hynde and Siouxsie Sioux took part in the gig and the esteemed British director Derek Jarmen (who's company made the 'So Young' video and who had directed three Smiths videos) hung out with the band afterwards. And in early September they picked up the coveted Mercury Music Prize for their album and then donated the £25000 prize money to cancer research (they were also busy that year supporting Youth Against Racism In Europe by donating 'The Big Time' to the 'By Any Means Necessary' LP and backing a Northern Ireland youth charity by contributing 'The Next Life' to a compilation called 'Peace Together').

Fate, however, had plans for Suede over the coming months. On August 11th The Drowners was released as the first US single and on September 12 they skimmed the Atlantic once more to join The Cranberries for a six week tour. Already strained by the backlog of touring the band were hit by tragedy right at the start. In New York Bernard heard that his father had died and flew home immediately. When he returned a week later he was in no mood to be playing the 'old' set of songs night after night.

The touring side of the band had always grated with Butler who saw it as a waste of time that could've usefully been spent in the studio. To make matters worse The Cranberries 'Dream' had just turned into a hit in the US. On the back of album sales of 300 000, Dolores and co were turned into the main attraction and with grunge rock at it's zenith Suede found themselves fighting for attention. Very little was right with that tour. Butler later told Guitar magazine **"There were things within the band, like people getting off their faces on days off - I wasn't in a very good state of mind and it all kind of disgusted me. Sometimes it was fine but sometimes it made me feel sort of dirty."**

While the rest of the band flew between dates, Butler stayed with the crew on the bus, sitting for long highway hours in the lounge writing for the next album and mulling over his future. In Las Vegas his alienation from the rest of the band and the 'on the road' lifestyle got to the point where he was completely unable to leave his hotel room. In the end, despite healthy reactions in some citys (Bowie turned up for the Academy show in New York) Suede cancelled the end dates of the tour and flew home early, striking out a set of European shows due to "exhaustion". Butler explained the early end to the tour more graphically **"The reason we came home early was more to do with the fact that I nearly went insane,"** he said.

The signs of a band under pressure were apparent when Suede gave a November press conference for a group of fans to accompany the launch the Love And Poison video. Butler was edgy and quick to criticise the film's director. The mood amongst the band was dour. Brett told the NME's John Harris that he'd rather be living on the West coast of America than dealing with his sniping, cynical home country and his one liner comment "England drives me nuts" ended up on the paper's cover. At the time it seemed like a U turn for a band who'd made much of their inspirational connection with English street/bedroom life. But as well as the band's own internal problems, there were background events affecting their feelings about the UK. Brett's rival Damon was making much of his own Englishness in the Cockney-esque new Blur tunes, and pop parochialism in the form of a nascent Britpop scene was beginning to spread.

"That was just to wind up loads of people who were getting all Little England-ist at

me," explained Brett later. **"I was just getting sick of it. Every fuckin paper and magazine cover I saw myself on they put a picture of a flag behind me. And I just found it really nationalistic. Everyone wanted us to be this figurehead of English culture and perhaps they saw us like that but I never intended it to be like that, and certain lesser bands decided to take on the mantle once we'd rejected it, and fair enough. But I never wanted it so I started winding people up saying I didn't like England and I wanted to move away. People were doing my head in, making preconceptions about what I was and what I wanted to do in my life. There was a lot of the lyrical content of the last album (Dog Man Star) was based around that. Once we'd created this blueprint, which I think a lot of people followed afterwards, of writing about small situations, idiosyncratic situations, it started a cartload of other people doing a similar thing. Whether it was a direct influence or not, I'm not saying I wrote that therefore a load of people copied it, a load of people probably hadn't even heard the fuckin' album, but once I'd done that I wanted to do something completely different. In a sense the next album was a bit of an about face on that. I didn't want to be pigeon-holed so I wrote a song about James Dean and this that and the other."**

Do you think Noel Gallagher having a union jack on his guitar is distasteful?

"Not really. I find that quite unpretentious. So it's OK. I don't find it particularly contrived. I think there's other bands that couldn't get away with it. It's such a fine line isn't. You just know Oasis can go and play with Union Jack guitars because their songs aren't all about being some stupid little version of Englishness, they're a bit more universal, that's fair enough."

Stepping outside their creative cradle for the first extended period changed the band dynamics

irrevocably. They had proved everything they set out to in the preparatory years and now the choices were wide open. Against the on-going babble of contention that continued to surround them (the letters pages of the press were full of seething letters about Brett's traitorship and Simon Gilbert was doing his bit with his 'underage' gay sex revelations) they played a pair of French shows and a December secret gig at London's LA 2. There were new songs in the set, and one of them stood out like an AK 47 rifle at a vicar's tea party. It was called 'We Are The Pigs' and it was a right little doomy onyx flamethrower.

chapter three
the wild ones

the wild ones

Hurtling across the clear North American sky at 400 miles an hour, Brett Anderson wakes from a dream. The seat in front of him comes into focus and still in the grip of the subconscious anxiety he remembers where he is. He's on a day flight across the Nevada desert on the way to yet another American gig. The band are scattered around the aircraft and everything seems normal, but he can't shake off the residue of his panic-y nightmare. Remembering some of the somambulent events, he taps his old schoolmate Mat Osman on the shoulder and recounts his vivid dream about a kid called Little Boy. "Little Boy?" says Mat. **"That was the name they gave to the nuclear bomb that was dropped on Hiroshima."** Out of the window Brett can see the vast expanse of desert wasteland and in the distance there's a mushroom shaped cloud of smoke. Rationally, he knows it's just a fire out there, just a coincidence. But the dream and the feeling of unease stays with him.

When it came time to write the second Suede album Brett was no longer escaping from a narrow life. The shackles of suburbia, poverty, London life and bigotry were no longer on him but as the restrictive walls came down he began to feel a type of generalised insecurity. The world travellers sense of global tension was with him. He started to recall the feelings he had as a kid when the threat of nuclear war underpinned news headlines. He was no longer simply one of a comfortable gang of London sybarites. Even the grounding familiarity of his Notting Hill one bed had gone.

Fed up of being bombarded with fans and phone calls he'd moved to a large, dark, Gothic style house in Highgate and gradually the atmosphere of the new abode began to permeate the writing. He'd wander the garden, looking up at the rooms outside his section of the building which used to belong to the Menonites religious sect. Few people bothered him, and he was free to fantasise, fire up his senses, and let his imagination wander. As well as "living in the last century" he was involved in an all consuming relationship with a girl. It's rumoured that during the Highgate days her parents used to refer to Brett as 'The Vampire'.

"I did get very isolated and started writing in a very isolated way," he recalls. **" I think that album was pretty much a love song to the same person. So it was a very personal thing, pretty much all the words were about the same person, and it didn't include anyone else."**

Brett had decided that the second album was going to be an epic masterpiece. Despite the fact that there was little communication between him and Bernard Butler there was at least

some synchronicity in their attitude to the next record. Butler wanted grand, six or seven minute songs too. For a while the pair could survive as a songwriting-by-post team.

Nine months had gone by without Suede releasing a single. In February the newly lauded Manchester band Oasis were arrested on a ferry crossing to Europe adding to their growing reputation as heroic rock'n'rollers. Elastica and Blur were starting to take over the news pages of the music press and the whole poppy hyper-confident, Britpop scene was moving up a gear. Suddenly Suede had a host of younger rivals and prior to the release of 'Stay Together' on Valentines Day in February the 'backlash' word was being whispered louder than ever.

'Stay Together' was however a towering, ostentatious wonder of a song and it completely silenced the backstabbers by going straight to number 3 in the charts. Butler had worked on it while his father was dying, pouring his emotional trauma into his playing. Anderson had written the nuclear sky darkened words while haunted by fears of apocalypse and disintegration. The combined effect was awesome, and on one of the B-sides there was further evidence of Brett's (brave) new world vision. 'My Dark Star' embodied the global politics of 3rd world countries vs the rich white power in the shape of an Indian girl *"She will come from India with a gun by her side..."*.

The side effects of travel (he'd taken a holiday in India at the start of the year) dislocation, substances and stardom were clearly on the surface when 'Stay Together' came out. Brett talked about new song 'We Are The Pigs', explaining it as a rallying cry for the disposed with apocalyptic, panic in Highgate overtones. Specifically he said he was imagining the homeless tramping up the hill to gentrified Highgate and *"crushing the skulls of the clergy."*

There was something distinctly Orwell-ian about Anderson at the start of 94. 'Orwell's '1984' is one of the few books he's ever admitted to admiring. As if to confirm his mood, at the start of the February British tour, Brett and Simon were pulled over by the police while driving back from a gig in Worthing. The officers who stopped them revealed that they knew the band's name in advance. Clearly they were looking for something and the speculation in the Suede camp was that Brett's open-ness about drugs had made him a target.

As winter thawed out into spring a sombre cloud sat over the pop world. In March Kurt Cobain overdosed on heroin and went into a coma in Rome. In April the news of his suicide cast a solemn shadow over music. No-one was taking themselves lightly in the following weeks. Suede meanwhile had re-convened in Kilburn's Master Rock studios to record their second album, bringing Butler and the rest of the band back into daily contact. The writing by post phase was over, and now the four of them, and producer Ed Buller who'd worked with them from the start, had to find common ground.

Steady progress was made for the first couple of months but gradually the level of

tension built up. Butler and Ed Buller were not seeing eye to eye on the overall sound of the record and old gripes between Brett and the guitarist were coming to the surface. In April Brett put a brave face on things, telling Melody Maker

"The songs I write on my own are always very musical and very melodious and well written and structured and all that but they haven't got the extra sparkle that we get when I write with Bernard." But by May Butler was disgruntled enough to give a rare interview to Vox in which he made clear his dissatisfaction with the teamwork. **"Brett's so fucking slow it drives me insane,"** he said. **"It's difficult for Brett to get around anything that isn't ABC. He doesn't surprise me alot."**

When the interview came out the atmosphere in the studio took a dive. Butler was pushing for even longer more grandiose songs than Brett had envisaged. The mixing desk faders were being yanked up and down with increasing violence. Eventually the antagonism came to the surface (it's rumoured that Butler wanted Ed Buller off the job, and delivered an ultimatum to Brett) when at the end of May Bernard took two days off to get married.

The band were not invited to the wedding and except for a brief return to pick up his guitars, Butler never came back to the studio. Eventually, after a couple of days uncertainty it dawned on the rest of them that he had gone forever. After the weeks of bad blood, it was almost a relief and they celebrated in the studio, getting the three man horn section to join in with an improvised version of 'The Girl From Ipanema'.

Fortunately for the band the album was mostly finished by he time Butler left. They were however in the glaringly invidious position of owning a dozen swoonable new tunes with no guitarist to help play and promote them. Butler's departure remained a dark secret for five weeks until Phil

Savidge finally broke the story on July 10th. The music press leapt into gear writing anxious cover stories asking 'Is It All Over For Suede?'. For a while there was even a question in Brett's mind as to whether they could carry on.

"We decided to carry the band on and we changed the line up and we'd made the decision based on the feeling that the band was a lot more than the sum of it's parts. I felt that there was a spirit to the band that should carry on, and I made that decision instead of calling it a day with Suede."

Was that a consideration?

"Yeah at the back of your mind it's got to be. I'd be lying if I said it wasn't. Of course there's an option there. Of course something has died about the old formation of the band because one of the ... blokes has left. I'm not going to start lying about that. But I made the decision and we promoted the album. It was kind of like playing a load of cover versions almost. Even though I'd co-written the songs and they were completely written down the middle between me and him. There was no excess of power on either side, they were *completely* co-written songs in every way. But it did feel like we were playing cover versions because it was like a former life. It was history. And I wanted to get on with the new stuff. It's difficult when you're playing some bloody festival in Finland and you're knocking out the old tracks and you're just thinking 'Fucking hell I can't wait to get back home and carry on writing'."

It was a surreal new scenario for Suede. Legal letters were being exchanged between Butler and the band, and they'd been forced by a law suit from a folk singer who been using the name for

years to change to The London Suede for America. The band felt confident about the quality of the new album but everyone in their camp new that Butler's departure was the perfect opportunity for the long delayed Suede backlash to flood in. It was important that they found a new guitarist quickly. Bernard Butler had relocated to France to work with Julianne Regan (the project didn't work out) dumping an entire third album's worth of Suede material before moving on to his solo project with David McAlmont. Suede meanwhile placed an advert in the music press for a new member.

Before the advert had even hit the press the 17 year old Richard Oakes had seen the news announcement of Butler's departure and sent in a tape of his guitar work. The precocious strummer from Poole in Dorset had played in a series of school bands. His dad had taken him to see his first gig - The Fall in Bath - and turned him on to The Clash, and he'd been a Suede fan for years. His local group The Electric Daffodils had made a bit of a name for themselves, but the chance to be involved with Suede was too magical to let pass by.

Up at Nude Records Simon Gilbert walked into one of the offices and found Brett listening to a tape of what sounded like early Suede demos. **"I don't remember us doing that"** Gilbert told Brett. The reason he didn't recall the demo was because it wasn't

Suede. "No. This is a guitarist," said Brett. "He's 17." The tape was from one Richard Oakes and it came with an accompanying letter saying that he would write the band's next album for them. A couple of supercool auditions later and Oakes had dropped his A levels and was in the band.

According to Mat he had "absolute confidence the confidence of being good". The babyfaced Oakes was not only completely in touch with the Suede sound, he also had the right baby-faced good looks and the firmly grounded personality to deal with the sudden star trip. When asked to join the band he replied "Hmmmm. I suppose it's better than school." In a fairy tale scene his parents saw him off on the train to 'start his new life as a rockstar'. The announcement was made on September 17th.

With the band's doubters casting aspersions about their ability to carry on with a new line up, they were by now in belligerent mood. No-one at the label wanted 'We Are The Pigs' released as the first single from the new collection of work. It was too abrasive and the title was hardly a radio jingle. But they insisted and 'Pigs' came out complete with yob-art B-sides 'Killing Of A Flashboy' and 'Whipsnade' and a scarily Brave New World style video, settling at number 18 in the September charts. Despite the spectre of long difficult months touring the new songs without Butler, Brett was publically confident. "I feel ridiculously thick skinned about wanting to be in the music business," he told the NME in September. "I don't feel fragile about it at all. There are people who want to put this fey image on us but I feel incredibly rooted in it."

The perennial Suede difficulty with prioritising their own muse rather than following the herd instinct had again put them 'up against it'. Blur's 'Parklife' was setting a jaunty cockney pop tone for the year, Pulp were taking suburban camp to the tabloids and the broadly conservative rock of Oasis's 'Definitely Maybe' was cleaning up in the charts. A loose Lad Rock coalition was coming together and Suede's

intense, vaulting, highly strung new songs were no more part of it than they were members of the Adidas-lite Sleeper, Elastica, Shed 7 grouping. As if to emphasise their maverick status they announced the arrival of the new album by graffiti-ing the title 'Dog Man Star' outside the offices of the major music and listings magazines.

"I like having a certain amount of distance from everything, and I think it shows in the music," says Brett. **"I don't think there's anyone else who makes the sort of music that we make. I certainly don't have any ambitions to make the music that any of my contemporaries are making. I feel as though all the rest of them are trying to make one sort of song and I'm trying to make another sort of song. And there's not much intermediate space where we meet, and I like that."**

'Dog Man Star' may have looked isolated in 94 but its isolation was nevertheless splendid. Released on October 10th, its provisional titles 'Sci Fi Lullabies' and 'National Anthems' hint at the contents. An excessive hour long symphony of baroque guitars and cirro stratus stings, it soars lyrically away from the kinky backstreet Engishness of the first album into a cinematic world of riots, nuclear paranoia, Hollywood stardom, warped love, rock'n'roll tragedy and drugs. The opening automaton stomp, 'Introducing The Band', is worthy of a re-energised Pink Floyd, 'Heroine's Marilyn Monroe reverie is carried by exquisite guitar shards and 'The Wild One's' (the title borrowed from the Marlon Brando movie) glides on a sublime melody.

A mood of doomed romance presides giving a tragic tint to both the personal and the global themes. In 'The Power' Brett's imagination reaches out beyond the pebble dash drives to Asia and Africa, and rails against the predicament of the powerless. In 'New Generation' he's swinging with the E-generation kids and sinking into an uncontrollable love affair and again in the comedown ballad 'The Asphalt World' a drug fuelled relationship takes centre stage. As a reflection of Anderson's inner world it implies a far from tranquil soul, wrestling with the painful dualities of love, drugs, power, travel and stardom, but still being able transform the highs and lows into majesterial pop. The sweeping orchestral neo-West End musical style end piece 'Still Life' couldn't be more affirmative.

According to Brett, the startling sleeve image of a naked man stretched out on a bed in his garret was chosen because "it's sad and sexual I think, like the songs." The photo by 70s German photographer Christian Vogt was not however Brett's first choice. Plans to use use a shot of a male body with a female face, on it's hands and knees and wearing a dog collar were thought to be too confrontational by the record company.

To coincide with the album's release Suede set up a fan club only show at London basement Raw club on October 10th. Richard Oakes had already officially made his live debut in Paris, but it was his first performance in front of the sceptical British press. After forty minutes of astounding grace under pressure there was no-one in the room who doubted his ability to fill Butler's shoes, certainly as a player. Suede sounded tougher than before and there was a manic, aggressive edge to Brett's

performance that would remain through the 'Dog Man Star' tour and become part of the band's permanent character. The album went to Number 3 in the charts, and for the rest of the year they hit the road, ploughing through British, American, Japanese dates and in Europe teaming up with the only contemporary band with a similarly adrenaline hearted spirit, The Manic Street Preachers.

From a point of near death, Suede had come back fighting . The album was a virtuoso riposte to the Brit-boppers. Oakes was a little miracle. Brett had even hit on a neat joke put down of Liam from Oasis who he'd referred to as "the singing electrician". 'The Wild Ones', the second single from the album made it to number 18 in November, but more importantly it showed that the new member Oakes was clicking into place. Extra track on the CD with the 'Introducing The Band' Brian Eno mix - 'Asda Town' - was the vinyl debut of Oakes and it sounded sharp. Seeing out the year with a fan club show at London's Heaven in December the band appeared to have come through their difficulties in style.

There was however a sizeable and highly unwelcome rumour dragging at their heels through the end of 94. In the October edition of iD Damon Albarn had told the interviewer **"I know for a fact that Brett is doing heroin".** It was mud slinging of the worst sort, but there was little that Anderson could do. He had already discussed the subject in public earlier in the summer and made it clear that **"I am not a heroin addict".** There was no more he could add. Later Brett pointed out :

"There are lots of people who have said things about the way I live my life which have been completely inaccurate and libellous. There's lots of times I've been on the phone to my fucking lawyers and said 'Blah blah blah' and then it ends up being this 'Well hang on if this happens it's going to kick up more dirt than it's worth'. But sometimes you feel like it yeah. There's a lot of bitter little people out there that are after your blood and don't care in what way they get it. They should get their wrists slapped and it's quite frustrating sometimes. "

The frustration was exacerbated at the start of 95 when the NME joined the band on their British tour. Suffering from flu and somewhat road weary Anderson was dragged out to have his photo taken at 9 in the morning, and the resulting shots of a bedraggled, tired looking Brett were used on the front cover with a caption 'Is It All Too Much For Suede?' While accepting that the band were on fine gigging form the journalist John Harris raised the heroin question only to be told firmly by Anderson that he was not a user. Anderson had never denied that drug use was sporadically part of his lifestyle. 'The Living Dead' from the B-side of 'So Young' deals specifically with the demise of a junkie. But the speed with which the vultures gathered at the hint of a good rock tragedy story was depressing to behold. Anderson felt set up.

" I think I'm incredibly resilient actually," he said. **"They had a little angle that they wanted to sell a couple of copies of the paper on. That's the thing about the manipulation of the media, it is incredibly easy. For that story all they needed was a couple of shots of me looking like a bag of shit and it was easy. The story writes itself doesn't it. No, I'm incredibly resilient. A bit too resilient at the end of the day because I have this ability to pick myself up all the time. Nothing really gets me, because it's the music I'm after. It's this quest for what I want."**

For a man on the edge Brett had a surprisingly busy first half of 95. The 'Dog Man Star' tour ran through to the midsummer. 'New Generation' brushed the singles chart top 20 in January and the first songs written with Oakes (on a days break from touring) -'Together' and 'Bentswood Boys' emerged as b-sides. In February, Brett joined the legendary singer of Serge Gainsbourg's 'Je T'Aime', Jane Birkin for a duet. The pair recorded 'Les Yeux Fermes' for a French AIDs charity album. And an American tour took the band through to April where they teamed up with support group Strangelove in Europe. Despite the necessity of playing songs from the 'old' line up of the band, morale was good and the now tension free Brett and co socialised with Strangelove more than they had with any other support band. Perhaps it was the 12 hours they spent together stuck in the free bar of a broken down Swedish ferry.

The fruits of Bernard Butler's collaboration with ex Thieves singer David McAlmont were beginning to appear (including a tune called 'You Do' which was originally written for Suede) but Brett was himself busy stretching beyond the bounds of the old Suede. On French TV he duetted with Terence Trent D'Arby singing Neil Young's 'Cinammon Girl'. And night after night on stage he pushed the physicality of his performance further and further. From the foppish sexual flaunting of the early days the band had turned into a mean rock thrills machine. Blur might have won the sausage dog lovers vote, filling Mile End stadium with that summer's pearly king act, but at The Royal Albert Hall and later at The Phoenix Festival Suede were the real diamond dogs. Not even a torrential downpour at Phoenix could obscure their hard edged radiance.

Two new songs were previewed in the charged up atmosphere of Phoenix - 'The Young Men' and 'By The Sea'. After the trauma of losing half the writing team the quality of the new tunes proved that the band had plenty of glories ahead.

"To say that I just came up with the lyrics is really vastly underestimating what I did on the early songs" reflects Brett. **"It's one of the things that I think history has got wrong about the early part of Suede. There's much more than that. All the vocal melodies that I write are hugely instrumental in the actual musicality of the songs, and I think my musicianship is something that I always underplayed for political reasons on the first two albums and now I'm not willing to underplay it."**

"I've never had a problem about songwriting and I've never had writer's block and felt I can't write. At first it was quite scarey. Because Suede have been together now for seven years, we've been in the limelight for three or four years - and you learn how to write songs with people very well, and then you get chucked in the deep end like that and the whole way that you write music and approach music is completely turned upside down. But at the end of the day if you can turn it around and make it work it's incredibly good for you, it's really great. Because you're not in this situation where you're cotton wooled, nurse-maided. You're having to make it work for itself. I thought Suede was getting to a period with 'Dog Man Star' where certain sides of it were getting obscure. And it was relying on the fact that it was just Suede doing it and therefore it would be good. But with the next album I felt that the songs really had to speak for themselves again."

chapter four
star crazy

star crazy

As the summer of 95 faded, residents of some of London's less chic perimeters might have observed a lone young man strolling the streets in a vaguely distracted condition. While the shoppers bustled by and the bunked off school kids ran for the nearest park, the tall, towsel haired figure would move at a slower pace, slightly out of time with everything but the stirring litter. In one hand he'd be cupping a cigarette, in the other there'd be a dictaphone which he occasionally hummed or half-sung into. His petrol blue eyes would flicker with a benign proprietorial light. Sometimes he'd step off the pavement as if unaware of the traffic.

With the 'Dog Man Star' tour over Brett was back in West London. The Edgar Allen Poe like environs of Highgate had been left behind for a more human, sunny flat in Ladbroke Grove allowing Sphinx, his Persian cat to sunbathe in comfort and Brett to set about writing the next album in a more tranquil frame of mind. The turbulent relationship of the Highgate days with its physical fights and brick throwing episodes was behind him. He had a new girlfriend and his musical perspective was distortion free. This time round he wanted to write directly and colloquially. In consideration of his flatmate Alan and to avoid fights with the neighbours, he'd had one room soundproofed and for days he'd pace the padded mini-studio, working on ways to translate the chemically, sexually, joyfully intense lives of his small circle of friends into songs.

When inspiration wasn't coming he'd wander off outside, maybe head out to some forgotten edge of town, and record his free'd up melodies and thoughts into a dictaphone. Occasionally a mad night of getting high would kick him into the right frame of mind. He was taking the time to do some groundwork too. Saul Galpern from Nude was sending him records over. T Rex's's 'Tank' made a big impression for the first time. He'd never listened much to Bolan in the early years when critics were fingering him as a glam rocker and in the same way, after years of being told that there were similarities, he finally started listening to Scott Walker. Brian Eno's early edgey solo pop also took a good few spins on the CD player. This time round he wanted the kind of simplicity and gleaming metal hooks that cut through even while you were doing the ironing.

By a coincidence of instincts Richard Oakes was meanwhile putting together tunes in a bristling, sweetly vicious fuzz rock style. Brett would come over and sing him vocal lines. With surprising speed they put together 'Trash', 'She' and 'Saturday Night' and as soon as they were written the mood picked up. At last they knew for sure that the Anderson/Oakes team really could produce a great album.

NFIEZ-NOU
TRE BRONZ

"I suppose he is younger than me and I'm more experienced than him," says Brett, considering the chemistry between the two of them. **"But the reason why we picked him to be in the band was because, he might be physically young, but he just isn't young. He can handle anything. He's a sixty year old man inside a twenty year olds body, that's pretty much how I see him. He's much older than the rest of us and he's got strong ideas about how his songs want to sound. I think the whole question of his musicianship is really going to take off on this album because he's done some brilliant stuff on it."**

While Oasis and Blur fought it out in the tabloids, Suede kept out of things, steering a steady course towards a blinding third album. In September they released the live video set 'Introducing The Band', and that month they came together to record a cover version of Elvis Costello's 'Shipbuilding' as their contribution to the Bosnia charity album 'Help' but otherwise they were a camouflaged presence. The desire to lay low for a while was intensified in October when Simon Gilbert and a friend were attacked by a gang of anti-gay thugs leaving a pub in Stratford. The attackers put both of them in hospital and though their assailants were unaware that Simon was in a band, nobody was in a hurry to rush back into the limelight.

With Christmas approaching the band booked rehearsal time in Dave Stewart's studio in Crouch End. The sessions were relaxed and nobody thought much of it when Simon Gilbert's cousin, Neil Codling started coming down to the studio to hang out. The twenty one year old Codling had finished a three year Drama degree at Hull University and was living near to the studio and looking for auditions to attend. There was however something very appropriate about Neil's skinny, nonchalant, reptilian presence looking on as the band worked on the new songs. Brett instinctively took to him and since they knew he could play a bit it seemed natural to invite him to contribute. At a run through of 'By The Sea' occasional keyboardist Oakes had to play guitar, so Brett asked Neil to sit down at the piano. Immediately it was obvious that he belonged.

"This guy just turned out to be this amazing all round musician," recalls Brett. **"And he actually integrated himself into the band to such and extent that he started writing songs with us. He's becoming a real key member of the band who's opinion I can trust incredibly. And he's got a really brilliant overview about music. And he's an incredibly talented musician. He talks about musical technicalities that don't even enter my head. So it's great."**

After a Christmas break the band got back together for a fan club show at London's Hanover Grand on January 27th. The set was all new, the atmosphere was electric and to ecstatic response from the fans Brett now had an androgynous, icy, 3D pin-up backing him up on vocals and playing keyboards. Codling's cold blooded glamour acted as an aesthetic thumbs up for the band. Suddenly they were more defined, more Suede, and the less Neil actually did the more the younger kids loved it.

By the end of the year 'New Boy' had his own fanzine and was a complete hit with the teen press, introducing Suede to an audience they'd previously fought shy of.

The recording sessions for the album took place at Townhouse, Mayfair and Master Rock studios and ran through to May. Ed Buller was again producing and this time there was a genuine togetherness in the studio. As the songs racked up, crackling with energy and bursting with city joyrider euphoria the character of the new album shone through. It would be up. It would be pop.

It would be in love, in lust and in the city. Someone suggested that they should call it 'Ultra-Suede'. In the end however they settled on 'Coming Up' and on July 29th teed up for the album release with first single 'Trash' (b/w 'Europe Is Our Playground' and 'Every Monday Morning' or 'Have You Ever Been This Low' and 'Another No-one'). The song was the perfect Suede bounce back tune, with fierce guitars, a cascading ultra-bright melody and a quintessential Anderson lyric celebrating the resilient romance in being "....traaa-aaaaa-ash you and me/We're the litter on the breeze/We're the lovers on the streets...".

The street kooks took to the day-glo sounding, all black clothed new Suede like fashion victims in a New York thrift shop and after a year and a half of no Suede releases, 'Trash' frizbeed straight to number 3 in the charts.

"It's a really important song," says Brett **"I wanted it to be really communicative, really unpretentious, and really just honest. None of the words in it are particularly obscure. They're all just sort of 'Maybe it's the clothes we wear'. It's just a very simple romantic song. 'We're trash'. But it's a positive thing."**

"I don't feel as though I have to dissect it to find anything particularly beautiful. It's not like trying to find some sort of obscure beauty in it. It's more finding a positivity in something that's shit rather than trying to find the Byron-ic beauty. I try to look at it like that. I feel as if I've grown up in that way. I'm not searching for some sort of Aubrey Beardsley, wonderful opium addict stance on life at all. It's a lot more real than that I think."

Do you feel like an excited young person?

"Yeah totally. I definitely don't feel like an adult. I know everyone says that. You get these old dears who get to 60 saying 'I feel the same as I did when I was 21'. But I don't feel in any way jaded by life at all. I refuse to be jaded! I refuse to end up as some bitter old git worrying about something years and years ago. Yeah sometimes you wake up and think 'Fucking hell!'. But I've never woken up and thought 'I'm going to go and live in Hong Kong'."

The new Suede seemed completely rejuvinated. Anderson was looking fit, lithe and healthy and talking to interviewers about Neil's brown rice diet rather than any current chemical phase. Oakes and Codling had given them both a songwriting shot in the arm and a longer term youthfulness. Codling even joked vampirically that they were going to replace Mat with two 14 year old girls whose blood they could feed on to keep them young. Osman himself told Melody Maker's Simon Price that

"our records have always had a balance between joy and darkness and that shifted a bit on this album just because we were happier."

On September 1st Suede played a midnight gig at Virgin records and as the working week crawled out of bed 'Coming Up' popped another vitamin pill and sprang out of the shops. The tunes were less snooty, more instant and coated in yobby amounts of saccharine and the setting was firmly back with the disaffected lovers and lifers of petrol fume clogged rainy townscapes. As the sleeve shot (of Models One face Lee Williams stretching his synapses on a mattress) implied, the task of eroticising low rent life was far from completed. 'The Beautiful Ones' extended the 'Trash' theme of celebrating the club kids and the crazies. 'Lazy' tripped off into the imaginary world of two gently mashed lovers. And 'She' turned voyeur on a sinister female presence. The T Rex influence came through loud and clear in 'Filmstar' where Brett lets his movie junkie side pass through the screen. 'The Chemistry Between Us' (written with Neil along with 'Starcrazy') extrapolated the 'Asphalt World' theme of hyper stimulated love into into a glorious seven minutes. And the mellifluous 'Saturday Night' swung out the door with its best clothes on and a straightforwardly romantic spring in its step.

"The way I write is that unless when I've finished a song it actually turns me inside out, it doesn't see the light of day," says Brett. **"So all of that criticism about 'You've said that bit**

before' seems completely irrelevant'. I repeat myself, yeah but who doesn't. I actually repeat myself deliberately sometimes. I quite like having a set of words that are almost your palate, like an artist would have a set of colours that he uses all the time. If other people use them now it'll be 'Oh that's a Suede phrase' like a 'Suede person'."

'Coming Up' was the sound of Suede realising what they do best and doing it with ruthless genius. It went straight to number 1 in Britain and made a greater dent around the world than any of their previous albums. In all sorts of obscure parts of the world they were now 'the biggest band'. And in the UK they were no longer just a huge cult. The whole pop scene had changed. Compared to 91 the quality of the bands in the mainstream had gone through the roof. They were younger, brighter, more confident, and more to the point it was Suede who'd shown them the way.

"The mainstream moved. We didn't," commented Mat, succinctly describing the Pied Piper phenomenon of Britpop. Bret however had slightly more to say. **"It's a more personal thing with me,"** he explained. **" Because I feel that Suede are quite seriously responsible for a lot of it in lots of ways, good or bad. I'm not saying that it's a wonderful thing to be responsible for, like a cure for cancer or something. I think it's perpetrated some abysmal music. I think it's perpetrated some pretty good music as well. But I do feel quite close to it. Strangely close because we're not part of the pack, but I do think that Suede kind of initiated it by virtue of our existence, the kind of songs we were writing two years before anyone even thought of the term Britpop."**

The cool thing about the Brett-pop band that toured Britain and Europe from September, playing three triumphal nights at London's cavernous Roundhouse in December and blazing on through to January 97, is that they're still in many respects a young band. At the Roundhouse there was no generational gulf between them and their chosen support acts, Subcircus, Placebo, Jack and Strangelove. And the three post 'Coming Up' singles 'The Beautiful Ones', 'Saturday Night' and March 97's 'Lazy' present just some of their strengths. With the new young guns on board, Mat and Simon re-enthused and Brett feeling absurdly confident, they're potential is still unfolding before us. There's a whole other side to Suede hinted in less radio trashing new tracks like the dark and drifting 'Europe Is Our Playground' and the spacey 'Every Monday Morning'. As Brett pointed out 'Coming Up' is a 'stepping stone' for the new band. The future's their's for the making.

"We've never been in anyone elses slipstream, we've never been particularly running with any crew and so we've always had to forge our own way," says Brett. **"We've always had to make our own mistakes rather than rely on other people in the gang to make mistakes and that's just the way it is, that's the way I like it."**

"Part of the problem with Suede has been that we've never bothered drinking with people and going to those places and

so people don't really know what we're like. So they have this image of us as.. phhh... I don't know what. And they get told lies by people and they assume that we're quite evil, unlikeable people. I don't particularly care about being likable at the end of the day but you do get a false impression of people."

Do you think you're evolving as a person, progressing into new areas?

"Yeah. I do see that quite a lot. No. I think I'm regressing quite a lot. I think that's what being in a band does to you I think. You get to a stage where suddenly you get in this band and you do have to start living your life backwards a bit. I don't know why. I think you become less of a rounded human being the more you have to deal with, cause you have to be selfish really and if I'd never been in a band or never picked up a pen or guitar, or whatever, I'd probably be a much more rounded and nicer person. But you have to deal with so many fucking things and you have to be quite hard at the end of the day and have to be quite firm and quite uncompromising about what you do, so that it does actually alter the rest of your personality. So yes, I'm regressing."

If Mat left now Suede would almost be your solo project.

"It would mean I was the only member from the start yeah. I mean me and Mat and Justine and Bernard formed the band in 1988 or something like that and I guess two of those have gone now, but I don't really think of it like that and I don't really want it to be thought of like that. It's a band that goes through a lot of changes but that's the way it is. It's not a solo band at all."

"I'm not a solo artist in the slightest. I like being in a band. And you know, the band are fundamentally important to the sound, Mat and Simon, much more than the credit that they're given. Not just musically but in terms of the whole feel of the band. They're not just these two people that we phone up every two weeks. Their opinion is vital. I couldn't take one step unless the rest of the band loved it. It's not some dictatorial situation at all. I'm firm friends with all of them and we're all equally good friends. It's just that I focus it all and that's what I do. So I do feel a good thing about the future of it yeah."

Could you exist comfortably outside your current lifestyle?

"No I'm completely addicted to it. I could never exist outside of it at all, if I was going to be completely honest with myself. Even if our next album sold fifty billion a round the world, I couldn't live in some castle or something. I'd just go mad. I do really need to write. I've always scribbled, since I was about five years old. But I've always thought of myself as a songwriter, because the ideas I've had have never been purely lyrical ideas. I've always come up with tunes and words in exactly the same quantity. And it's perfectly suited to me."

"You have to be a bit of an all rounder to be in a band. It's weird. You have to be able to deal with absolutely every side of it. You have to be a politician, a fuckin' orator, a musician, you have to be this that and the other, you even have to be a fuckin accountant. It's like being a fuckin housewife! Five thousand things you have to be excellent at to be any good at it. And I'm quite suited to that really. I'm quite good at dealing with lots of people. At the end of the day I can sort out the things that are important and ignore the things that aren't. I'm very seldom wound up by press and stuff because I know it's just a big game. It winds me up for about ten minutes and them I'm fine. Part of the game.

You've got to deal with it. It's like going down a snake when you're playing snakes and ladders, and then you throw another dice and you get up to the top again. That's the way it is."

How do you think Suede fit into Brit culture at the moment. You could say people will remember the 90s for Oasis, laddism and the Lottery. Where do you intersect with all that?

" I really don't know. I really don't know how you compete with fashion. Because I think it's probably too huge a force to compete with. You either are sucked into it, you manipulate it because it fits in with your own personality, or you just ignore it. I feel as though we were sucked into fashion in the early days and people will remember 92 or 93 as something, something and Suede. And from then on you can't really ride the horse, because you just turn yourself into some sort of fuckin' caricature of yourself. It's something very few people can do.

"Someone like Bowie was able to do it because he was a solo artist, so him and Abba were the 70s, or something. But I don't know how you penetrate those things. It's something I really don't want to have that much of a grasp of. It gets to be too scarey. You start pretending to be someone you're not and

that's something I have no intention of starting to do. I think you've got to exist *between the lines*."

So are you happy to exist in your own little world?

"No, that sounds incredibly condescending, but I'm sure you don't mean it like that. But I know what you mean. It's all you can hope to do isn't it. It really is. Everyone wants someone to be this huge omnipotent string puller and at the end of the day people are just like pieces of driftwood on the tide... litter on the breeze."

On a summer's afternoon Brett picks up his black leather jacket, swings it over his shoulder and walks out into the altered state of London. Whatever dramas are kindled, whatever scandals snag them, and however much the popscene changes around them nothing can destroy the enormity of Suede's accrued meaning. It's bigger than any of them now, even bigger than Brett. It's a bright idea. A clear vision. A weighted word. A way of living amidst the love, poison, drugs, wars, sorrows, highs, fashions, clubs, fears, hopes and beauty of the here and the now. And all of that from five letters. All of that from six undressed kids. From underdogs, to men, to the stars.